Firebird

Also by Em Strang

POETRY

Bird-Woman
Horse-Man

FICTION

Quinn

Em Strang

Firebird

Shearsman Books

First published in the United Kingdom in 2024 by
Shearsman Books Ltd
PO Box 4239
Swindon
SN3 9FN

Shearsman Books Ltd Registered Office
30–31 St. James Place, Mangotsfield, Bristol BS16 9JB
(this address not for correspondence)

www.shearsman.com

ISBN 978-1-84861-939-5

Cover image: Meinrad Craighead, 'Artemis With Burning
Coyotes,' 2004. Copyright © Amy Dosser.
meinradcraighead.com.
Used by permission.

CONTENTS

The Spark

The Flame

The Fire

The Ashes

For Mary

The phoenix is an archetype of every age, inherent in the experience of fire; for we will never know for certain whether fire derives its meaning from images of external reality, or its power from the fires of the human heart.

—Gaston Bachelard

THE SPARK

The Ash Tree

In the morning, we stand beneath it like flowers
– common wood sorrel, maybe –
or walk beneath it like strays.

It agrees this season is one of promise
and plenty – enough birds for every branch,
enough breeze to allow every leaf.

Sometimes a whole army of ants
walks here, teeming, working
towards some perfect, nameless hill.

In the evening, it rises in the woods –
tall trunk, limbs, pale green keys,
those first fruits of summer swelling.

We stand here hungry for everything,
as though there's nothing left to ask for.

The Sad Fate of Rooks

Once upon a time there was a sun
burning in a blue sky.

It stayed there all day
and then disappeared at night.

Nobody knew where it went
or who put it out.

When the only sun died
the owls started up,

hooting with sadness
at the end of the world.

Hours passed or was it foxes,
marking the path between now and then?

It rose again because of the rooks –
they're the ones who hauled the sun back.

We made the earth! they cawed,
We made the sun!

But the sun got fed up
and burnt them to blobs.

The Sun Thieves

When the sun comes up
we grab it and shove it in our satchel.

It's hotter than we thought
and so powerful it makes us wonder.

The satchel is struggling,
bulging and smoking at the seams.

Sometimes a flame emerges
and licks the satchel's face,

sets the strap on fire. The satchel
must know its time is up.

We listen to it strain
against the hot might of the sun.

We walk one brave mile
with the satchel ablaze.

The leather has caught fire –
the old hard skin of the animal

burns up readily, easily,
and the sun sucks it to nothing.

It's obvious the satchel no longer exists
and the light of the sun has blinded us.

We're walking, or believe we're walking,
and the sun is rising on someone else's world.

The Sunroom Shoulders the Burden of Light

The sunroom knows how to be still,
to allow exposure corner by corner.

There's an old armchair
and a solar lamp that's always lit.

Something comes into the glass
body of the room.

To be the sunroom is to exist
in the sunlight of ages,

before the house was built
and after it crumbles to dust.

The Spark & The Horse

The spark is dozing on the track.
It's blown in from somewhere,
a single twinkly speck
like a bit of fallen star.

It wakes up almost out,
snorting on the empty track
like a sad old horse
in a lonely field.

It knows it could live for days
if the breeze fans it
into a blazing barn
or a conflagration of cornfields.

The north wind is the spark's lover,
so too the dry grass,
the bracken,
maybe even the track.

"What's missing?" says the horse,
"There's always something missing,

so the missing one can be missed."

Last Scrap of Trees

We walk out to the last scrap of trees.

The trees are spindles,
rooted in bedrock and dry springs,
honing their deep skill of stillness
or readiness for the gaping wound.

We're small animals with burnt faces.

We tell the trees we're sorry,
but it's not enough.

The Unmaking of Loneliness

A hidden woodpecker in the rain,
pock-pock in the drumming rain.

In one tree and then another,
everything – especially the world –
is drilled loose.

Each hollow is a cylinder of darkness,
unafraid, not waiting for anything.

A House Standing in Darkness

Out in the open, something old and dark
shakes out the glass from its frames,
blows wide the front door
to let more darkness in.

Somehow the house is both hollow
and full of darkness at the same time.

When we walk inside,
the hunger for something
outside the house – the quarrying – ends
and each footfall comes along by itself.

The whole house is bursting with darkness.

There are cupboards here and old sofas,
memorials with familiar names.

We sit in thought for centuries,
waiting to remember the sun.

It's true, the whole house cannot be pierced
with the silver pin of the mind.

If I Have to Cut My Feet

If I have to cut my feet in the desert
it's because I've abandoned my shoes,
left them lovingly, one beside the other,
in a room with a dark cloth at the window
that reminds me of my mother.

The shoes sob quietly so as not to disturb
the room, and the old smell of sand and hot wind
comes in to soothe the canvas uppers,
the worn rubber soles that know feet
better than light knows the sun.

This is not my choice, but it is.
My bare feet fret over the glassy crystals,
the blasted, eroding grains of quartz,
until every inch of tough, old skin is free.

Angle Shades

A single moth on the dark wood of the night table.
It's small, yes, because the house is big.
But the moth has eyes even the front door can't boast of,
minute black beads that perceive the human need to be held –
that vast golden cup, filling and spilling over.

It looks without flinching, lets itself be looked at in return.
It's like a barely vibrating leaf in a far off, untrodden forest.
Too easily it could be crushed or its body's dust smeared,
as the one coming in the front door at this late hour, climbs
    the stairs
and fails to notice the night table or the cup.

The Field

The field comes out at night
with its wide waiting and noiselessness.

Each furrow unravels itself
into the dark ocean of earth, the timeline
of everything hidden or hiding.

The field is never alone ′and knows
how kind the night is, to come so kindly
without fail, to sink down to its knees
unconditionally, to bring one field to another,
to bring the far burn invisibly to the river.

At dawn, hen pheasants slowly uncover
from hedgerows that no longer exist,
and the cock pheasants stand blazing
inside their own quiet fires,
like men who know how to love.

Mistle Thrush

The bird's speckled breast
opens into sunlit spirals,

into shawl upon shawl
of longing.

At midday in the larch woods
nobody sees the bird

except in the mind's eye,
that hungry bead scanning the trees

for something bigger than a thrush
and brightly coloured

like a bird of paradise
with an orange fountain for a ruff.

The Mirror

If you're strong enough to hear it –
the blackbird has flown into the house!
It's a hot, airless day and the back door
was left wide for the bird. It's indisputable,
the dark blue door, its open width
and the matt black of the bird's coat,
his burnt wings and sun-ringed eye.

If you're strong enough to hear it –
the blackbird has flown upstairs!
He has followed the smell of water
and is listening to the streaming light
from his perch on the lip of the sink.
Here he meets his double, meets his double
and dances for the benefit of all blackbirds.

He is looking and seeing, hopping and waiting
for the other to disappear or die.

Lonicera Vulgaris

Honeysuckle leaves have sprouted
and flourished along the side of a house.
So green, humans have to close their eyes
to imagine it, and even the long spring grass
is baffled. How to be a leaf
of such luminosity! How to sit so well
on a stem alongside others!

The leaves tenderly sway
in the slightest breeze, swaying, allowing,
as though their minds are made up
to affirm everything.

Here and there, humans
watch from small, rickety seats,
each barely visible to the other –
the grass is so tall.

The rooks easily outnumber them.

To learn such deep longing,
one must long for a long time.

Daffodils

It's March before you find the earth
ready for your good yellow,
for your loud, unabashed trumpeting.

You open the gate and speak of love
between the house and the road,
between the road and the woods
and in all the places winter has shamed
into silence.

It's March and a woman walks here
and there between your green stems,
herself a new flower.

Nobody speaks like this anymore.

The Western Mind

The western mind flies
straight through the window –
it knew it was open –
but doesn't see the trap:

endless grey desks and chairs,
rows of strip-lights and screens
with neither pollen nor nectar.

The mind buzzes from one thing
to another, then lands on the over-
full drawer of a filing-cabinet.

The desks and chairs pay it no attention –
they're busy melting in the April sun.

An unanticipated breeze quietly closes the window.

Brown Hen

Birds, all birds, possess a core of fire —Gaston Bachelard

What if the light doesn't want to hover between feathers
or slip impeccably from bird to earth
like it does in religious paintings?

What then?

Why did nobody say that the hen –
this russet one in particular –
is always more than its wishbone?

Who cares whether it presses its claws into the dark clods?

The clods care.

Linnet

You're not a linnet if you lie inside all day, breaking
the line between you and the kingdom of birds.
You're not a linnet, no matter how much you warble.
You're not a linnet because the way linnets move
is more surrender than prayer, more air than earth.

A linnet's limbs are lighter than yours and meant for
something altogether different, like linking one world
with the other – impossible without wings.

You're not a linnet, even if you dance in the woods
all night where they flock. They warble and watch,
but your forehead is not crimson enough
and you must moult at least three times
before making the crossing, moving the mind.

The Rope Between Worlds

My son, you are soaked wet to the skin, carrying a heavy gun
   – Mitsuharu Kaneko

All the mothers are pulling the rope in –

– even the men pull, hauling the rope into long, arcing
   loops, arm over arm –

– saltwater drips off them –

– the weight of it pulls them to their knees –

– the water is cold and clear –

– their limbs take to it reluctantly, like tired children –

– there's talk of late sun and a slow harvest –

– someone shouts the word wait! –

– it doesn't matter how many mothers or where they're from
   or what year –

– the men mutter to themselves like seabirds –

– when the water deepens, it shelves into darkness –

–at the end of the rope, a miracle – a creel of blazing fire.

Old Red Vase As Go-Between

The vase is old and red
and knows how to be a vase.

It has red eyes and red ears
and nobody is a better listener.

That's why we choose this vase
to put her flowers in.

The flowers – bluebells, forget-me-nots –
hold all the words she withheld.

Tight inside the petals and leaves,
each word is swaddled safe.

We listen to the leaves jostle
– the unspoken sparring.

They stay there for a week, mutter
a wild blue scent into the room.

Thank God the vase listens
to every last syllable and sob.

At night, when the room is a speech
bubble, we leave them alone.

The Veil of Rain

The veil of rain says, "Wear me!" So we put it on. Not one of
us dares discard it; nobody even pulls it back to speak. The
veil is breathtaking in its quiet cleverness: pitter-patter, pitter-
patter, as it streams over us, makes us not us. Sometimes it's so
heavy, we have to lie face down on the earth. We lie and doubt
for a long time, while the sun scorches the back of our necks
and shines all the way through to our throats.

Water of Ae

Don't wait to walk out along the back-roads
to the boggy fields where the swans are.
You can cross the river at the small bridge
and walk a walk you've walked for ten years
every day, even when the rain's on hard
and the wind's tearing at you. Don't wait
thinking you've seen it all already –
the flooded fields, the brown river,
the white swans. You can't see these things
from the bog-eye of the human. Don't wait.
Stride out with your boots on, or better still,
barefoot, and be inside the wind a while,
be inside the field like a grass halm might,
like a single blade awaiting sunlight.
Don't wait. Inevitably, it takes time
to unzip your hair, your skin, your face
enough to see swans, their blazing white,
but don't wait thinking you need better boots
or a waterproof that'll keep out the rain.
It won't. Don't wait. Walk out entirely
as though the mind is a rook's nest
in a tall, far off Scots pine and behold
for the first time, the swans, still there
after ten years of your looking, hunched
in the Scottish weather.
It doesn't matter how many similes
climb down from the rook's nest –
none of them fit. Don't wait.

Meeting God on an Old Stone Bridge

Afterwards a stone falls in,
hurrying to meet itself on the riverbed.

In a nearby flower shop, yellow roses
open in response to the light.

The bridge waits – lenient, unhurried,
carrying on in both directions.

The Alchemical Fire

Let the skin show itself at the throat.
Let the eyes move towards and away from.
Take everything off for the last time.
The sun comes in
and a small bird flies past.
Lift an arm, a hand.
Let the face tilt this way.
Someone's flesh is here and here.
The wind taps the glass once twice.
When the wind blows across the roof like this.

Crocus

This small flower opens
only for the sun.

On windy days it moves
in some new direction.

It speaks in *crocatus*,
a kind of yellowy hush.

The sun is its only true love,
even though the bees come close.

It knows it cannot outrun
time or darkness or snow.

In silence, a cup is being filled.

Snow

Beloved, the snow is swirling and I am
a single flake, falling. Each flake
alongside me sings as it falls
and I too am singing. The whole field
is big with song.

I look for you here, but there is no looking.
My eyes feel you instead, in the deep
roots beneath rock and grass,
where I have melted into us.

Us

Here in this deep pool
inside the old silver river
a single fish leaps
in the moonlight,
like a lover calling
her beloved.

All above the stars
are still and the water
is loose to her shape,
lapping, easeful,
or the river is a dream
of the eternal

longing to be whole,
a single multiverse,
caught between the banks
of one reality and the next,
calling and leaping
up

The Blazing House

It's too quiet for the house to collapse
and burn bright red in the half-light.
A big wide mouth opens
and closes over the scene like a candle snuffer,
douses the flames
for ten seconds, maybe eleven.

Who is being born tonight into this?

Eucalyptus Grandis

The oil is ready to burn.
It shouts across the valley
from the throat of every leaf.
After years of waiting
it wants to go up in glory,
to roar in the face of the hill
like a bomb.

The oil is crabbit.
It spends all day looking
for a spark, a glass bottle
in the dry grass or something
hot and violent like lava.

The oil refuses to give up.
It will think fire into being
and the world will witness
its personal conflagration,
its far-reaching smoke

until night comes
and swallows the hill whole.

The Brink

is the thrush tapping the snail shell

steadily, accurately, against white stone; is

this particular stone, set aside in the world

for this purpose alone, or so it seems; is

the speckled breast of the bird, his wings

and straightforward beak, tugging one world

from the other, tapping intermittent Morse; is

the time of watching, the dark dome of the eye

sating itself on the field, the low river; is

THE FLAME
after Caravaggio

Martha & Mary Magdalene

The flame wishes to be touched. Whose hands are listening?

It flickers and spurts, testing the air like a fledgling swallow. It's a narrow bulb of heat and light, surrounded by darkness.

The room is saturated with colour – red, green, gold – and this is what the flame illuminates. It knows better than any how to flare up brightly and blaze; how to surrender its mutable, vulnerable form to the inferno.

There's nowhere to go in the dark, and even when the flame whispers, it shocks the ears and flabbergasts the hands, until they open beyond opening.

For centuries, the flame spoke only of orange blossom and scarlet silk and the missing tooth of an ivory comb. It spoke *lentissimo* of the density of wood, the reassurance of a table down the ages, of the women who leant there, laid down an alabaster dish or a sponge, something low and light to remind the table of its weight and height, the leafy integrity of its origin.

Here in the Venetian mirror of our times, the flame speaks of the dark in a tongue we pretend we've forgotten.

Still, one woman dares to walk twelve miles in the dark to the crossroads at the far edge of town –

What's lit can't be unlit.

The Burial of St. Lucy

She traverses centuries, taking with her the heart of every human who ever loved, polishing them in eternity, sanctifying the valves and chambers before returning them to their owners: there's still much heart-work to be done.

To inter so much feminine beauty into the soft rich earth is to remember the gift of timelessness – we're neither now nor then but both at the same time, patient with the necessity of mystery.

Our hands clasp softly, loosely at the belly. We know there's nothing we can do to stop time unless we lose it altogether from our lives; drop it, as though it were a crozier or a walking-stick upon which we lean too much.

To inter so much feminine beauty is to celebrate the surrendered life, in which the flame burns forever and cannot be put out.

Even inside the colossal bodies of the gravediggers it nods, waiting, and inside the man of armour and the man of the cloth. Inside the grieving women, the dark heart of the flame grieves too – its soft hiss insists on our ears and clings to the throat.

Only the heart knows that the soft ochre of the earth and the soft ochre of the towering catacombs speak as the flame speaks: as above, so below.

It's the orderly mind that blinds us.

The Taking of Christ

Let the one that is the armour defend himself with metal over metal, until being beneath metal is unbearable, so dark that he must lay himself down in the dust. Let the one that is the armour move metal plates not meant for movement. Let the one that is the armour congratulate himself on the completion of his task.

Let the one that is the furrowed brows of Christ sink down to his knees and sob. Even when there's no sun, let this one feel the sun's rays. Let this one feel the full weight of the sun in his eyes, the searing light across millennia. Let the one that is the furrowed brows of Christ sink down before rising up.

Let the one that is the lantern be lit. Let the one that is the lantern tilt the flame until it burns brightly. Let it shine upon him, spilling light until nothing is left in the dark but darkness.

The Calling of St. Matthew

Outside, the streets burn. The awning of every shop and tavern has been destroyed and is hanging in shreds or drifting in the air as ash. The inbye land is burning. The fields are red with fire, hot orange and bright white as though heaven and hell have come together as one. The trees burn like torches, sending flares up into the sky: the time is now.

Further out, beyond the towns and cities, the land is folding beneath fire. The wind has fanned the flame for forty miles and only a fool walks barefoot on the earth. All the way to the coast, the land is blackened, a burnt crust for extinct birds.

Inside, the men are pointing. To point is to beckon attention. To point is to signify and to clarify. Are we pointed at? Do we point?

The boy's bright tunic refuses to go outside. It'll barter everything to stay where it is, to be comforted by the familiar, to secrete itself in the folds of its sleeves. It watches everything – the open ledger, the inkwell, the young man fiddling with coins.

Outside, all of Rome is burning. Inside, the other, older flame.

Mary Magdalene

If somebody is hiding it's not immediately obvious. The
pearls have been scattered, removed in preparation for their
transformation. All pearls become something else in time.

The one hiding has taken off her clothes and is laying them out
carefully on the ground. She folds the brocade, meticulously
smoothing the edges and letting her palms and fingertips feel
the cool silk of the cloth. She lets one tear fall. Then she lets
another and another until every father, sister, mother and
brother has been torn from the hem of her. She does not falter.

The white chemise fills the room with a parachute of light.
She kneels down to lay out its voluminous shape, arranging
the sleeves and the body of the fabric until it looks as though
a woman is still wearing it, as though her heart is still beating
beneath it.

She rolls up the small red sash and places it beside the pearls.
She has displaced nothing.

To be a woman now is to feel the full weight of her feet on the
earth. Everything touches her – the air, the quiet colours of
the room, the human eye – but nothing can touch her now.
The flame burns inside her blood-strong darkness.

Stillness can only be done to us.

Supper at Emmaus

The cockle has waited a long time for this. It's come from a world so far removed from the linen tablecloth, the plucked and cooked hen, the basket of fruit, that it understands resurrection without having to ask a single question.

It is a milk white ear, snapped loose from its other half, emptied, consumed, bringing with it the sound of the sea and the smell of brine. It knows how to listen. It speaks in susurrations, to remind itself where it comes from.

It doesn't know how to doubt. It's adaptable, even as ornament – a broken bivalve adorning the heart of a seeker – and belongs to no one. It knows who it is, what it's made of and where it will return to.

It's possible to touch the rough ridges of this sturdy shell; to hold it up to the nose and inhale the smell of the Adriatic or the Mediterranean, seas which have birthed cockles for millennia; seas which once teemed with fish – mullet, bream, turbot, bass, whiting, sole.

It's possible to cup the broken bivalve in the palm; to witness its delight in being concave and convex at the same time. It boasts of nothing but whiteness, as it presses a small light into the flesh. It appears empty on the inside, but its clean shell remembers its meat well, and in remembering is saved again and again.

It's possible to take the innocent shell and give it to someone we hate, someone who does not believe what we believe, does not live the way we live, someone who sees darkness where we see light. We give the broken bivalve to the hated one and they give us the other half in return.

THE FIRE
after Craighead

Burning Crow

Cruciform crow –

the small bones of the wings
(humerus, radius, ulna)
tap into everything,

the infinitesimal boundary
between fire/no-fire

or how the heavens reside
equally everywhere

if you've marrow enough
to look.

The small bones look
and look,

hopeful, humble,
extending themselves

beyond the confines
of their form,

searching under burnt bushes
and hostile black trees

for the surging of light,
unconditional tenderness

and love.

Most birds' bones
are hollow, like flutes.

Arched Flight

The fire is inside the penis,
red hot and persistent.

It's the kind of desire that never gives up,
no matter how many lifetimes it serves.

It surges inside the coyote
from the tip of its tail to the tip of its tongue.

It's not coyote desire that's become
the charred remains of creatures

and the ash their bodies make,
the crumbs and flakes

that sing a funny little song
of something not yet born.

Raven ~~Death~~ Birth

The first black eye of the raven
came down from heaven
cloaked in a cottonwood leaf.

It saw the dark earth of the woods
and the bright sky above, burning
with a light it longed to return to.

The eye lived by light alone, basking
in the sun's rays, opening its single lens
as wide as the sun itself, shunning all shade.

It lacked nothing, needed no one.
It inhabited the woods feverishly,
hid beneath leaves when the fire came.

Birds Falling

They're not birds anymore –
they're getting ready to be oil.

Once upon a time the fire burnt them
and their bodies fell to the ground
like small empty stones.

Some stones are full and heavy and talk a lot –
they know how things get laid down.
They talk about eras as though Eras
is their middle name. They wait
a very long time for the truth.

Once upon a time the fire burnt the birds
and the birds lost their earthly lives.
Not a single feather mourned, not a single bone.

But the tiny bird hearts inside
the twiggy cage of their bodies
leapt about on the woodland floor,
dodging the sparks and hot embers,
pumping themselves full of whatever life
they could get, even when it meant
the agony of burning valves
and smoke-filled chambers. Even then.

This is the slick truth
the full and heavy stones speak of.

Wild Dogs Fleeing

Coyote flesh lives a guffawing life
from the first myocytes
to the muscle's last stretch.

It guffaws in the least likely places –
the hot pits of coyote legs,
in the ruff and the rump.

If you listen with the right kind of ears,
you can hear the waggish chuckle.
Even as it pounds with blood,

hot and straining,
the flesh is droll, each ligament
raucous with laughter.

It knows something we don't.
It must know something
we've neither thought nor dreamt.

One muscle jokes with another muscle
and together they circumnavigate the world
of the burning woods

beneath the hot pelt of the wild dogs.
Miraculous flesh!
Wise, thirsty, desperate flesh!

Some bright spark asks what's so funny
and the flesh says, "This!"

Coyotes Pass a Burning Tree

The forest lost its mind at first light.

We ran to find it
before it was too late,
but the forest was running too
and nothing can outrun
a running forest.

Had it stuffed its mind
inside the burnt hollow of a tree?

Had it hidden it
in the rubble of a shattered boulder?

Had it outsmarted us all
by burying it in ash?

We sighed
our last sighs,

and just before it was too late,
one of us gave up her mind

to the forest
in a quiet gesture of love.

Artemis with Burning Coyotes

On the first day, there's a volcano.
Lava enters the skin of the neck,
slips open the trachea, the jugular vein.

On the second day, there's longing,
the kind that turns men into coyotes
and coyotes into dead coyotes.

On the third day, there's the mouth
of the goddess champing on fire.

The mouth has come a long way down the ages
to arrive here with a full set of teeth
and a tongue that lashes the world
with a single, everyday word.

What word?

The mouth devours everything.
Its lips begin and end in flames.
It gnaws, it gnashes
and it tongues the fire's heart.

What word?

Burning Coyotes

We let out the last air of us.

Above the burning hot scarlet we're running,
sloping between night clouds,
leaving behind our bodies as offerings.

We don't know what we're doing
without paws, heads, muzzles or legs.

We leave as though there's nothing
we need to take leave of.

We become seamless
in the way blood is seamless.

Nobody hears our souls lifting up,
their robust silence,
the way they float and rest,

       float and rest

like brave lilies on an open pond,

                          up and out

beyond anything like life,
deep into mountains that are not mountains,
to a sandhill that is not a sandhill
in the middle of which is a red bridge that is not a bridge.

We cross the red bridge or the bridge crosses us
and,   like strange birds in a new cosmos,
we pass over, giving back whatever gifts we have.

It is extravagantly dark here, until it is light.

Coyotes Disembowelled

Outside time, the coyotes are burning.
The coyotes are burning and bursting open.
The insides of coyotes are lapsing and slipping out
into the woodland inferno.

The fire is coyote red and coyote orange.
The fire is real and the insides of coyotes are real.

The things that happen are happening
whether coyotes like it or not.

The trees are crashing down and crushing coyotes
and gopher snakes and porcupines.
All the bushes are crushed and set on fire
and all the berries and leaves
and all the thorns of bushes are crushed.

The insides of coyotes are happy.
The insides of coyotes have been shut up
in the dark for so long, held in the tight
muscle of the animal, constricted, commanded.

This coyote freedom is delicious.
The insides snake across the woodland floor,
ooze and belch bubbles in the hot air,
expose themselves to the kiss of the world.

Coyote Tails Burning

In the rainy season,
the tails cannot imagine
this lusty blaze
inside the follicle
of each hair.
The tails swing
out together,
brother-sister tails
being run by
the animal body.
The tails are alone
and apart from
one another.
The tails are one.
Inside the will
of each tail,
a memory of fire
at the beginning
of time.
"This is where
we're going,"
sing the tails,
as they're laid out
and burnt clean.
Even the cartilage
is burnt to ash.
Then the tails rise up
in adoration.

Bosque Fire Shaman
In Memoriam Meinrad Craighead

A local child made this story up –
the one about the fire shaman walking a tightrope.

If you're still enough to listen,
you can hear the rope twanging and shivering in the heat.

There it is, look, stretched out across the burning treetops
like prayers trembling above war!

Hola, tightrope!
Hola, shaman!

The child says the shaman breathes with her feet,
inhales the hot, smoke-filled air and exhales the unbroken world
with every miraculous step.

She trots the tightrope as though it's a wide, empty road.
There she goes, soothing from hot edge to hot edge.

The child says she's a vessel for lost souls,
a glass of holy water tilted at the lip of tomorrow.

THE ASHES

Firebird

I

Once upon a time there was a double miracle.
Nobody believed it but everyone knew it to be true.

It took place on a Friday or perhaps every Friday,
as the great bird appeared in a burst of flame.

The wings were tremendous curtains of fire
and the throat was a flute made only for song.

We knew the inferno would be quick and happy,
since this is how freedom tends to be.

We watched as the tail went up before us,
this fabulous bird incandescent with faith.

A quiet heaven fell as a small hill of ash,
the tilth of a being who knew how to die.

Those of us sleeping gave birth to the doubt –
that horrible weight in the twist of the gut.

But the fledgling arose – we watched it together –
from the ash of forgiveness and the embers of grace.

II

And then I realised that I'm the fire.
But the fire – is not me.
Although at the same time, I'm the fire.
 —paraphrase, Daniil Kharms

Come into this (im)perfect timber forest
to look at the (un)broken man, the one

who's put the fire out
or thinks he has.

Watch as he stamps the pit
in his black boots, cursory,

spitting at the embers,
his heart nested in the ash,

waiting
(as a fledgling swallow waits).

The sun throbs inside his head,
a thick dunt like a drunken fist.

For forty miles in all directions
the trees too are waiting

and the river is
a lisp between boulders.

Even if he prayed for rain – he won't –
it wouldn't fall.

Watch how the fire comes
to unzip the man –

a conflagration
in which he receives himself:

bull, raging butterfly,

double miracle
of flesh and spirit.

Watch him begin again,
the bird in his chest screeching.

III
After George Seferis

That whole night we were full of misery,
my God, how full of misery!
In the end, cavernous hearts, black guts, the trauma of ages
pumped into our sluggish blood.
Men with cocks as cruel as crowbars
broke down the women and broke down the children,
splitting them in half, taking them away from themselves forever.
Nobody heard us crying, calling.
The moon too was cut in half and the sun never rose.
The whole night and the whole morning
we were full of misery,
all light kept in shadow by the murderers.
Do you remember their laughter – how full of death!
Then the sun came, or something like the sun,
a vast explosion of light and heat
in the shape of a bird beyond our imagining.
We stopped crying, stopped calling
and lay down on the waiting earth.
The bird shone all of creation into being
before the men could stop it, after the men
had wept. *Inexplicable*, you said, *inexplicable*.
I don't understand people:
no matter how much they drown in darkness
they hold this unquenchable fire in their hearts.

Notes

'Water of Ae'
The Water of Ae is a tributary of the River Annan, Dumfries &
Galloway. The name 'Ae' likely comes from the Old Norse word *aa*,
meaning 'water, river'.

THE FLAME is a series of prose poems in relationship with a num-
ber of Caravaggio's religious images – painted between 1595 and
1609 – and the global wildfires of 2021/22.

THE FIRE comprises eleven poems in relationship with eleven of
Meinrad Craighead's Bosque Fire paintings, images made in 2004
in the aftermath of a devastating fire in the bosque, the woods on
the banks of the Rio Grande near Albuquerque, New Mexico, where
Craighead lived. The cover of this volume features her 'Artemis With
Burning Coyotes'.

Acknowledgements

Thanks and acknowledgements are due to the editors of the following publications where some of these poems or earlier versions appeared: *The North* ('Burning Coyotes'), *Oxonion Review* ('Mary Magdalene', 'Birds Falling'), *Northwordsnow* ('A House Standing in Darkness') *Pushing Out The Boat* ('Angle Shades', 'The Unmaking of Loneliness'). 'Water of Ae', 'The Field', 'The Blazing House', 'The Mirror' and 'Lonicera Vulgaris' were commissioned for *Antlers of Water*, ed. Kathleen Jamie, 2021.

'Water of Ae' was also published in *100 Poems to Save the Earth*, eds. Zoë Brigley & Kristian Evans, 2021.

'Snow' and 'Us' were published in *Gitanjali & Beyond: The Unity of All Things*, ed. Bashabi Fraser, 2021.

'Burning Coyotes' was selected for the Scottish Poetry Library *Best Poems of 2022* Anthology.

'Firebird' was published in *Elementals (Fire Volume)*, Humans & Nature Press, eds. Nickole Brown and Craig Santos Perez, 2024.

Thanks also to the Hawthornden Fellowship and the Royal Literary Fund Fellowship, both of which enabled me to finalise this collection.

With special thanks to Amy Dosser for permission to use Meinrad Craighead's 'Artemis With Burning Coyotes,' 2004, as front cover image.